BETSY *Ross*

SPIRIT
of America®

Betsy *Ross*

PATRIOT

By Vicky Franchino

The Child's World®
Chanhassen, Minnesota

7

BETSY *Ross*

Published in the United States of America by The Child's World®
PO Box 326 • Chanhassen, MN 55317-0326 • 800-599-READ • www.childsworld.com

Acknowledgments

The Child's World®: Mary Berendes, Publishing Director

Editorial Directions, Inc.: E. Russell Primm, Emily Dolbear, and Lucia Raatma, Editors; Linda S. Koutris, Photo Selector; Dawn Friedman, Photo Research; Red Line Editorial, Fact Research; Irene Keller, Copy Editor; Tim Griffin/IndexServ, Indexer; Chad Rubel, Proofreader

Photo

Cover: Corbis; Art Resource, NY: 16; Corbis: 2, 22: Bettmann/Corbis: 13, 19; Joseph Sohm,Visions of America/Corbis: 14 bottom; Francis G. Mayer/Corbis: 15; Lee Snider/Corbis: 17; Shaun Best/Reuters NewMedia, Inc./Corbis: 23; Richard B. Levine/Newsmakers/Getty Images: 11; Liaison Agency/Hulton Archive/Getty Images: 12; Hulton Archive/Getty Images: 25, 26; Lambert/Hulton Archive/Getty Images: 28; Library of Congress: 20; North Wind Picture Archives: 7 top, 7 bottom, 8, 9, 14 top, 18, 21, 27; Stock Montage: 6.

Library of Congress Cataloging-in-Publication Data
Franchino, Vicky.
  Betsy Ross : patriot / by Vicky Franchino.
    p. cm.
Includes index.
Summary: Brief introduction to the life and accomplishments of American patriot Betsy Ross, credited with making the first American flag.
  ISBN 1-56766-169-6 (library bound : alk. paper)
1. Ross, Betsy, 1752–1836—Juvenile literature.
2. Revolutionaries—United States—Biography—Juvenile literature.
3. United States—History—Revolution, 1775–1783—Flags—Juvenile literature. 4. Flags–United States—History—18th century—Juvenile literature. [1. Ross, Betsy, 1752–1836. 2. United States—History—Revolution, 1775–1783.
3. Flags—United States. 4. Women—Biography.] I. Title.
  E302.6.R77 F73 2002
  973.3'092—dc21

2001007817

12   25   28

Contents

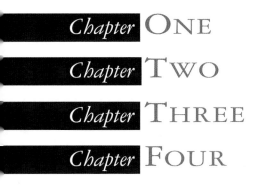

Chapter ONE

A Talented Seamstress

The first American flag

THE FIRST AMERICAN FLAG AFTER THE DEC-laration of Independence was made in 1776. The flag is an important symbol of the freedom and unity of the United States. Many people believe a young woman named Betsy Ross made the first flag of the United States. While no one can prove that Betsy made the first flag, we know she was a patriotic woman who loved her country.

Elizabeth Griscom was born in Philadelphia, Pennsylvania, on January 1, 1752.

She was the eighth of 17 children. Her family were **Quakers**. They worked hard and lived a simple life. Quakers did not play music, read novels, or dance. Their clothes and homes were plain. They rejected war and would not pay taxes to support it.

Betsy Griscom was born in Philadelphia, Pennsylvania.

Betsy, as she was called, attended a Quaker school. She went to classes six days a week. There, Betsy learned how to read and write and do math. She also spent time sewing. Betsy was a talented **seamstress**.

Betsy and her family attended Quaker meetings in Philadelphia.

7

When Betsy was 12 years old, her school days ended. At that age, most young girls stayed home and helped around the house. Her father, however, decided Betsy should learn a trade. He asked another Quaker to teach Betsy the business at his **upholstery** shop.

As a girl, Betsy learned to sew well.

At the shop, Betsy made friends with John Ross. John and Betsy shared a dream to open an upholstery shop of their own. Over time, their friendship grew into love.

When John turned 21, he opened his own small upholstery shop. Betsy and John wanted to marry, but there was one serious problem. John was not a Quaker. Quakers were not allowed to marry outside their religion. Betsy's family tried to convince her not to marry John.

But Betsy loved John and would not change her mind.

On November 4, 1773, Betsy Griscom married John Ross. After her marriage, Betsy was no longer a part of Quaker society. Many people refused to speak to her. That made Betsy sad, but she was strong and independent. She knew her own mind and did what she believed was right.

Betsy and John joined another church. Betsy found their services very different. They included singing and praying aloud. Betsy was used to silent prayer.

It was a time of change and trouble for Betsy—and for America. The future of the United States would be shaped in Philadelphia, the largest city in the **colonies**. Betsy Ross was there to see it all.

Interesting Fact

▸ The first postage stamp showing the flag appeared in 1869.

WE CELEBRATE THE U.S. FLAG ON A SPECIAL HOLIDAY CALLED FLAG DAY. We display the flag on June 14.

A schoolteacher named Bernard J. Cigrand first suggested a "flag birthday" in 1885. Cigrand organized his students at the Wisconsin Public School, District 6, in Fredonia, Wisconsin, to honor the American flag. He chose June 14 because the United States officially adopted the flag on that day.

Over the years, many U.S. schools and towns began to observe Flag Day. On May 30, 1916, President Woodrow Wilson officially established Flag Day. On August 3, 1949, President Harry Truman signed the National Flag Day Bill designating June 14 as National Flag Day. Today, communities throughout America celebrate this holiday with parades and patriotic displays (right).

Chapter TWO

Making the Flag

At that time, many colonists thought the British had too much control over their lives. The colonists wanted to vote on decisions that affected them.

On September 5, 1774, the first Continental Congress met in Philadelphia.

On September 5, 1774, representatives from the colonies met for the First **Continental Congress**. They put together a list of complaints and sent them to King George III in Great Britain.

Some of the colonists began to prepare for war against Great Britain. They were known as **Patriots**. Other colonists sided with the British. They were known as **Loyalists**. John Ross worked for the Patriots, guarding their military supplies.

On April 19, 1775, in Lexington, Massachusetts, fighting broke out between British soldiers and American patriots. The **Revolutionary War** (1775–1783) had begun.

In 1776, John was wounded and on January 21, 1776, he died. At only 24 years old, Betsy Ross was a **widow**.

John Ross sided with the Patriots, colonists who wanted independence.

After John's death, Betsy had to make a difficult choice. Should she keep the shop open or return to her family? The shop was a dream she had shared with John. Betsy decided to keep it open.

The war continued. George Washington, commander of the Continental Army, became

General George Washington thought one flag representing one country might help unite his troops.

Some historians say that Betsy Ross convinced Washington to use five-pointed stars.

frustrated that the colonies were not working together. He thought an American flag might help unite them. Who would make the flag?

Many people believe Betsy Ross made the flag. We have several reasons to believe this could be true. First, in those days, upholsterers often made flags. Second, George Washington's good friend—Congressman George Ross—was John Ross's uncle, and he knew Betsy was a talented seamstress. Third, Betsy's family remembered her stories about George Washington asking her to make a flag. Betsy was known to be an honest person. Fourth, written records prove that Betsy made many other flags over time.

The original flag had 13 stripes and stars to represent the 13 colonies. The stripes were white and red. The original flag design had stars with six points. According to

Betsy Ross's family, Betsy convinced George Washington to use five-pointed stars instead.

In this painting, Betsy Ross shows her flag to George Washington

For the colonies, 1776 was a year of many important events. On July 4, the Continental Congress approved the Declaration of Independence. The colonies were now independent from Great Britain.

The war was not going well for the colonies. People worried that the British would attack Philadelphia. Luckily, Washington and his troops kept the British out of the city. One of the most famous battles took place on Christmas night in 1776. That night, during a terrible storm, Washington crossed the Delaware River. His troops surprised the British and won the battle.

Around this time, Betsy renewed a friendship with a man named Joseph Ashburn. On June 15, 1777, they were married. The day before the wedding, the Second Continental Congress made the flag with 13 stripes and stars the official flag of the United States.

In this painting, General George Washington crosses the Delaware while one of his men flies the American flag.

Betsy and Joseph settled into their new life together. Joseph was a sailor who attacked and captured British ships for America. It was a dangerous job. Joseph was often away at sea for months at a time.

In late 1777, the British were very close to Philadelphia. Many Patriots, including Joseph, left the city. They could not risk being captured by the British. Betsy bravely stayed alone in Philadelphia to protect their home and shop.

To LEARN MORE ABOUT BETSY Ross, you might visit one of the houses she lived in with her first husband, John Ross. The Betsy Ross House, built around 1740, is on Arch Street in Philadelphia. Betsy Ross lived there from 1773 to 1786.

At the turn of the 20th century, 2 million people donated dimes to help restore that house. In 1937, the house was donated to the city of Philadelphia. Today, about 250,000 people visit the Betsy Ross House every year.

The Betsy Ross House has nine rooms. On the first floor, visitors can see the Flag Room and the Upholstery Shop. The family bedrooms are on the second floor of the house. In those days, families often lived and worked in the same place. Betsy Ross is buried in the courtyard next to the Betsy Ross House.

Chapter THREE

The End of the War

During the Revolutionary War, many British officers forced their way into the homes of colonists.

WHEN THE BRITISH CAPTURED PHILADELPHIA on September 26, 1777, life in Philadelphia changed. Many families were forced to share their houses with British soldiers. People were afraid to leave their houses. Food and firewood were expensive. The only people who weren't suffering were the British leaders. They kept on having elegant balls and fancy dinners. To survive, Betsy made dresses for Loyalist women and mended uniforms for British officers.

General Washington wanted to free the city. His first try failed, and many

soldiers were wounded or killed. The winter of 1777–1778 was terrible for Washington's troops at Valley Forge, Pennsylvania. They were cold and hungry all the time. The women of Philadelphia tried to help. They made clothing for the soldiers and gathered food.

By early 1778, however, conditions had not improved. Betsy had not heard from Joseph for months. She was worried. The British searched the area looking for hidden American ships. Luckily, they didn't find Joseph's ship.

George Washington at Valley Forge, where his troops suffered through a bitter winter during the Revolutionary War.

In June 1778, the British troops left Philadelphia. The town was free! Joseph finally returned home.

During the following year, life in Philadelphia slowly got better. The Patriots returned to the city. Soon, Betsy and Joseph had another reason to be happy—a baby! Their daughter, Lucilla, was born on September 15, 1779.

Betsy and Joseph's life was busy in 1779 and 1780. Betsy's business grew. Joseph was offered command of a new ship. While his ship was being built, Joseph decided to sail to the West Indies. Betsy was pregnant again. She worried about Joseph, but she was sure he would return before the baby was born.

Life at sea during the Revolutionary War was dangerous. This 1779 painting shows a sea battle between the Americans and the British.

Months passed. Betsy visited the docks to see if returning sailors had any news of Joseph. What she heard did not make her feel better. There had been terrible storms. Even worse, the British

In October 1781, the British surrendered at Yorktown, Virginia.

had captured many American ships. Betsy carried on as best she could. She worked in the shop and cared for young Lucilla.

On February 25, 1781, Betsy's second daughter, Eliza, was born. Betsy was overjoyed to have another healthy child, but she worried about Joseph.

Finally, in October 1781, the British surrendered to George Washington at Yorktown, Virginia. The Treaty of Paris ended the war in 1783. The United States had won its independence after eight long years.

Months passed. Betsy still hadn't heard from Joseph. Late in the summer of 1782,

Betsy learned that an old friend, John Claypoole, had returned to Philadelphia. John had been in a British jail, and Betsy hoped he had news of Joseph.

John Claypoole's news was not good. Joseph had been in prison with John. The British had captured them both and sent them to the Old Mill Prison in Plymouth, England. Conditions at the prison were horrible. Many men died of illness. Joseph was one of them. Betsy was brokenhearted. At 30, she was a widow for the second time.

Conditions in British prisons were often horrible with many people dying of illness before they could be executed.

22

THE FLAG HAS FLOWN THROUGHOUT America's history—in war and in peace. It has been taken to many places, from the world's highest mountain to the moon! The flying flag inspired Francis Scott Key to write the national anthem "The Star-Spangled Banner." Key wrote the song when he saw the flag still flying at Fort McHenry after a battle with the British in 1814. It told Key that the Americans had won the battle.

One famous photograph of the flag was taken during World War II (1939–1945). On February 23, 1945, U.S. troops planted the flag when they captured Iwo Jima in Japan.

Explorers often took the flag with them on their journeys. When Arctic explorer Robert Peary reached the North Pole in 1909, he planted a flag his wife had made. Barry Bishop was the first American to ascend the world's highest mountain—Mount Everest. He raised the flag there in 1963. In 1969, Neil Armstrong became the first man to walk on the moon. His flag showed the world that the United States was a leader in space travel.

The flag also flies at half-mast, or about halfway up, at sad times, such as the death of an important government leader. Only the U.S. president can officially order the flag flown at half-mast. In recent times, the flag flew at half-mast after September 11, 2001 (above). This was done to honor the victims who died in the terrorist attacks that day.

A Busy Life

▶ Shipmaster Stephen Driver first called the flag "Old Glory" in 1831. Driver flew his flag at sea for many years. Confederate soldiers were ordered to find and destroy the flag during the Civil War (1861–1865). Driver carefully sewed the flag inside a bed quilt to protect it!

OVER TIME, THE FRIENDSHIP BETWEEN BETSY and John Claypoole blossomed into love. But Betsy did not want to marry another sailor. She remembered the loneliness and worry she had endured with Joseph. Betsy told John how she felt. John decided that as much as he loved the sea, he loved Betsy more. He would find a job in Philadelphia.

Betsy and John were married on May 8, 1783. John had a new family—and a new job. He decided to work with Betsy in her shop.

While Betsy was happy with her new life, she still missed a part of her old life—her Quaker faith. She had loved the simple ways of her old religion. In 1782, some Quakers had formed the Society of Free Quakers. They were sometimes called the

"Fighting Quakers" because they had supported the war. Betsy joined in this new group.

The next few years were a busy time for Betsy. The shop grew and so did Betsy's family. In 1785, Betsy had her third daughter, Clarissa Sidney. In 1786, her fourth daughter, Susan, was born. That year brought sad times, too. Betsy's daughter Lucilla died and so did one of Betsy's sisters.

Betsy Ross kept herself busy in the shop.

The city of Philadelphia remained the center of the young nation. The **Constitution**

The U.S. Constitution was signed on September 17, 1787.

of the United States was signed there in 1787. In 1790, Philadelphia became the nation's capital. The city was busier than ever.

Betsy's family continued to grow. In 1789, her daughter Rachel was born, and in 1792, her daughter Jane. In 1793, an outbreak of yellow fever hit Philadelphia. Betsy and her family were frightened. Although her children were unharmed, Betsy's parents and one of her sisters died.

Betsy and John's shop continued to do well. Over the years, they moved to larger houses as their family and their business grew. In 1795, a move into new lodgings was perfectly timed. New flags were needed. Two states, Vermont and Kentucky, had joined the Union. And Betsy had another baby daughter, Harriet. Sadly, Harriet died just nine months later.

The new century brought changes to the young United States, and to Betsy's family. Washington, D.C., became the nation's capital in 1800. Philadelphia became a quieter place to live. That year, John's health began to fail.

In the War of 1812 (1812–1815), the United States fought against Great Britain again. Betsy's shop made many of the flags that flew on American ships. Betsy's daughter, Clarissa, and her niece helped Betsy through the war years. John's health got worse. John died on August 3, 1817.

Betsy decided to keep working in her shop. Work had helped her during the many sad times in her life. Betsy worked until she was 75 years old.

After she retired, Betsy lived with her daughters. During her last years, she became

In the War of 1812, the United States battled with Great Britain again. This drawing shows the Americans defeating the British on Lake Erie in Pennsylvania.

▶ Betsy Ross was an official flag maker for the U.S. Navy during the Revolutionary War (1775–1783). Records show that she was paid on May 29, 1777, for flags she made for the Pennsylvania Navy.

blind. On January 30, 1836, she died peacefully in her sleep. Today, she is buried beside John Claypoole in the courtyard next to the Betsy Ross House in Philadelphia.

In 1870, Betsy Ross's grandson, William Canby, made a speech telling his grandmother's story. Soon the story was in many schoolbooks. Although no one can prove that Betsy Ross made the first flag, there is no doubt that she was an excellent seamstress and true patriot.

Betsy Ross was a true patriot.

1752 Elizabeth Griscom is born in Philadelphia, Pennsylvania, the eighth child in the Griscom family.

1773 Betsy Griscom marries John Ross. They move to what is now called the Betsy Ross House in Philadelphia.

1776 John Ross dies, leaving Betsy a widow at only 24 years old. Betsy Ross may have created the first flag of the United States for George Washington.

1777 On June 14, the Second Continental Congress makes Betsy's flag, with 13 stripes and stars, the official flag of the United States. On June 15, Betsy Ross marries Joseph Ashburn.

1779 Betsy and Joseph's first daughter, Lucilla, is born. Two years later, their second daughter, Eliza, is born.

1782 Betsy learns from a friend named John Claypoole that Joseph has died. Betsy, 30 years old, is a widow again.

1783 Betsy marries John Claypoole. The couple works together in the upholstery shop.

1785 Betsy and John's daughter, Clarissa Sidney, is born.

1786 Betsy and John's second daughter, Susan, is born. Lucilla dies.

1789 Betsy and John's third daughter, Rachel, is born. Three years later, their fourth daughter, Jane, is born.

1793 Betsy Ross's parents and one of her sisters die during an outbreak of yellow fever in Philadelphia.

1795 Betsy and John's fifth daughter, Harriet, is born. She dies nine months later.

1800 John Claypoole falls ill.

1817 John Claypoole dies.

1836 Betsy Griscom Ross Ashburn Claypoole dies in her sleep.

29

Glossary Terms

colonies (KOLL-uh-neez)
Colonies are territories settled by people from another country and controlled by that country. When Betsy Ross was born in Philadelphia, it was the largest city in the colonies.

constitution (kon-stuh-TOO-shun)
A constitution is a set of basic principles that govern a state, country, or society. The U.S. Constitution was signed in Philadelphia in 1787.

Continental Congress (kon-tuh-NENT-ulh KONG-griss)
The Continental Congress was the group of men who governed the United States during and after the Revolutionary War. George Washington was a member of the First Continental Congress and the Second Continental Congress.

Loyalists (LOY-uhl-ists)
Loyalists were colonists who supported the British in the Revolutionary War (1775–1783).

Patriots (PAY-tree-uhts)
Patriots were colonists who were prepared to fight against Great Britain. John Ross was a Patriot.

Quakers (KWAY-kuhrs)
Quakers are members of the Religious Society of Friends. They are a Christian group that conduct simple religious services, wear plain clothes, and reject war. Betsy Ross was born into a Quaker family.

Revolutionary War (rev-uh-LOO-shun-ah-ree WOR)
A revolution causes a complete change in government. The Revolutionary War (1775–1783) was fought between the United States and Great Britain.

seamstress (SEEM-struhss)
A seamstress is a woman who sews for a living. Betsy Ross worked as a seamstress for much of her life.

upholstery (up-HOHL-stur-ee)
Upholstery is the covering on chairs and sofas. As a young woman, Betsy Ross worked in an upholstery shop.

widow (WID-oh)
A widow is a woman whose husband has died and who has not married again. After John Ross died, Betsy Ross was a widow.

For Further INFORMATION

Web Sites

Visit our homepage for lots of links about Betsy Ross:
http://www.childsworld.com/links.html

Note to Parents, Teachers, and Librarians:
We routinely verify our Web links to make sure they're safe,
active sites—so encourage your readers to check them out!

Books

Miller, Susan Martins. *Betsy Ross: An American Patriot.* Bromall, Penn.: Chelsea House, 1999.

St. George, Judith. *Betsy Ross: Patriot of Philadelphia.* New York: Henry Holt & Company, 1997.

Weil, Ann. *Betsy Ross: Designer of Our Flag.* New York: Aladdin Paperbacks, 1986.

Places to Visit or Contact

The Betsy Ross House
To visit the house that Betsy Ross lived in from 1773 to 1786
239 Arch Street
Philadelphia, PA 19106
215-627-5343

National Museum of American History
Smithsonian Institution
To see the Star-Spangled Banner
14th Street and Constitution Avenue, N.W.
Washington, DC 20560-0646
202-357-2700

Index